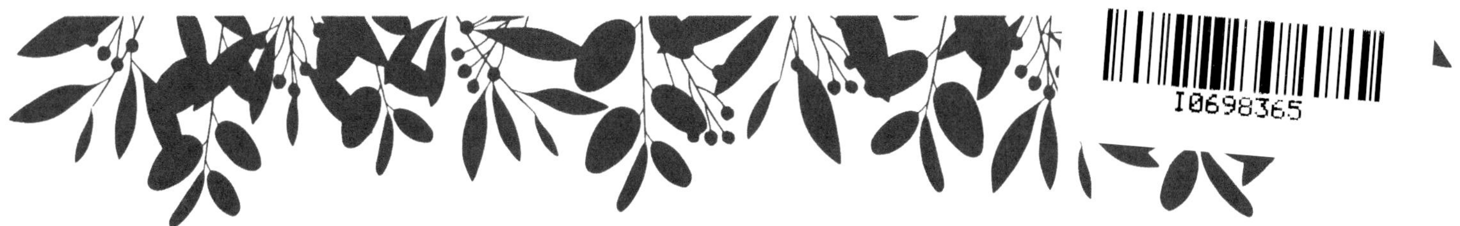

I am grateful to God for everything! And I believe that the meaning of life is to make sense of other lives. T.A., you are the meaning of my life.
Lov U

Sinara Hongaro

2024

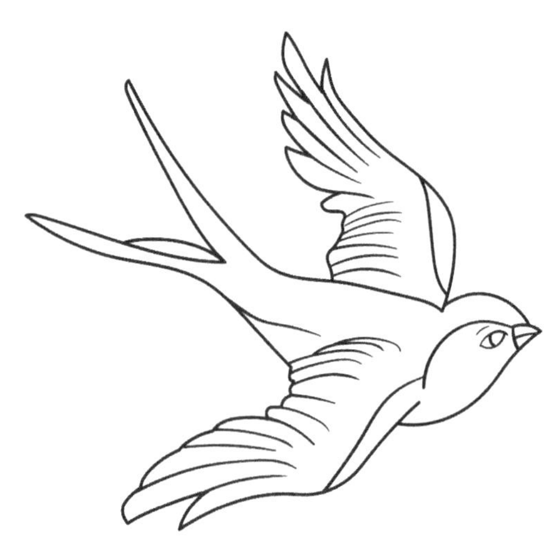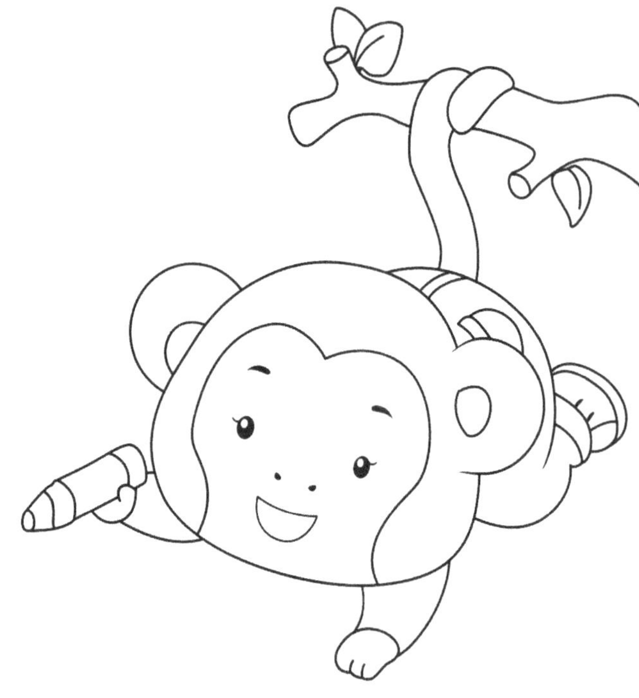

This Book Belongs to:

____

S.H.P.

Sinara's Hongaro Publications

ALL RIGHTS RESERVED ©
2023

No part of this publication may be reproduced, distributed, or transmitted in any form or by any means, including photocopying, recording, or other electronic or mechanical methods, without the prior written permission of the publisher, except for brief quotations incorporated in critical reviews and other specific noncommercial uses. Any unauthorized replica of this work is prohibited.

S.H.P.©

Sinara's Hongaro Publications

Test Color Page

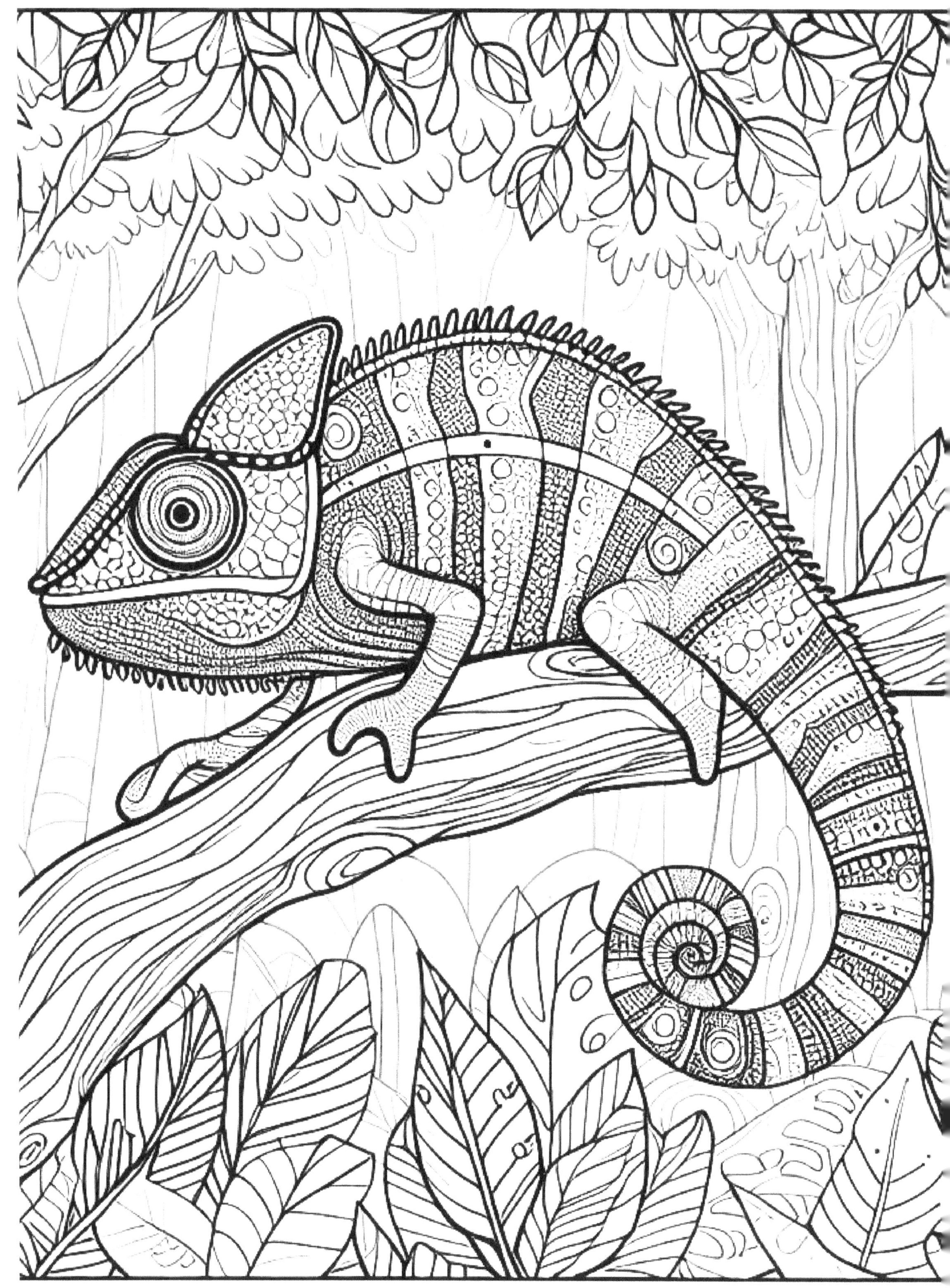

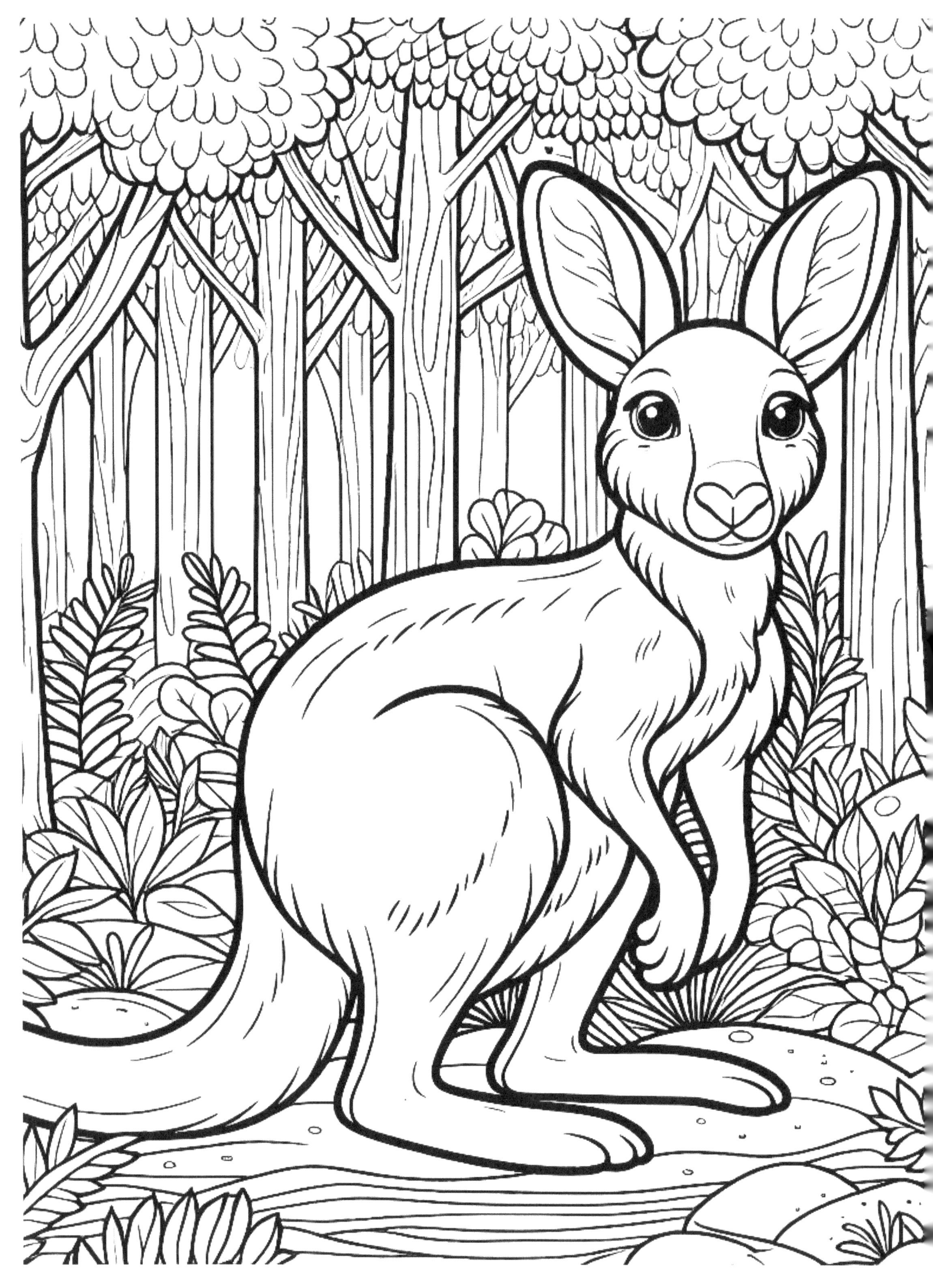

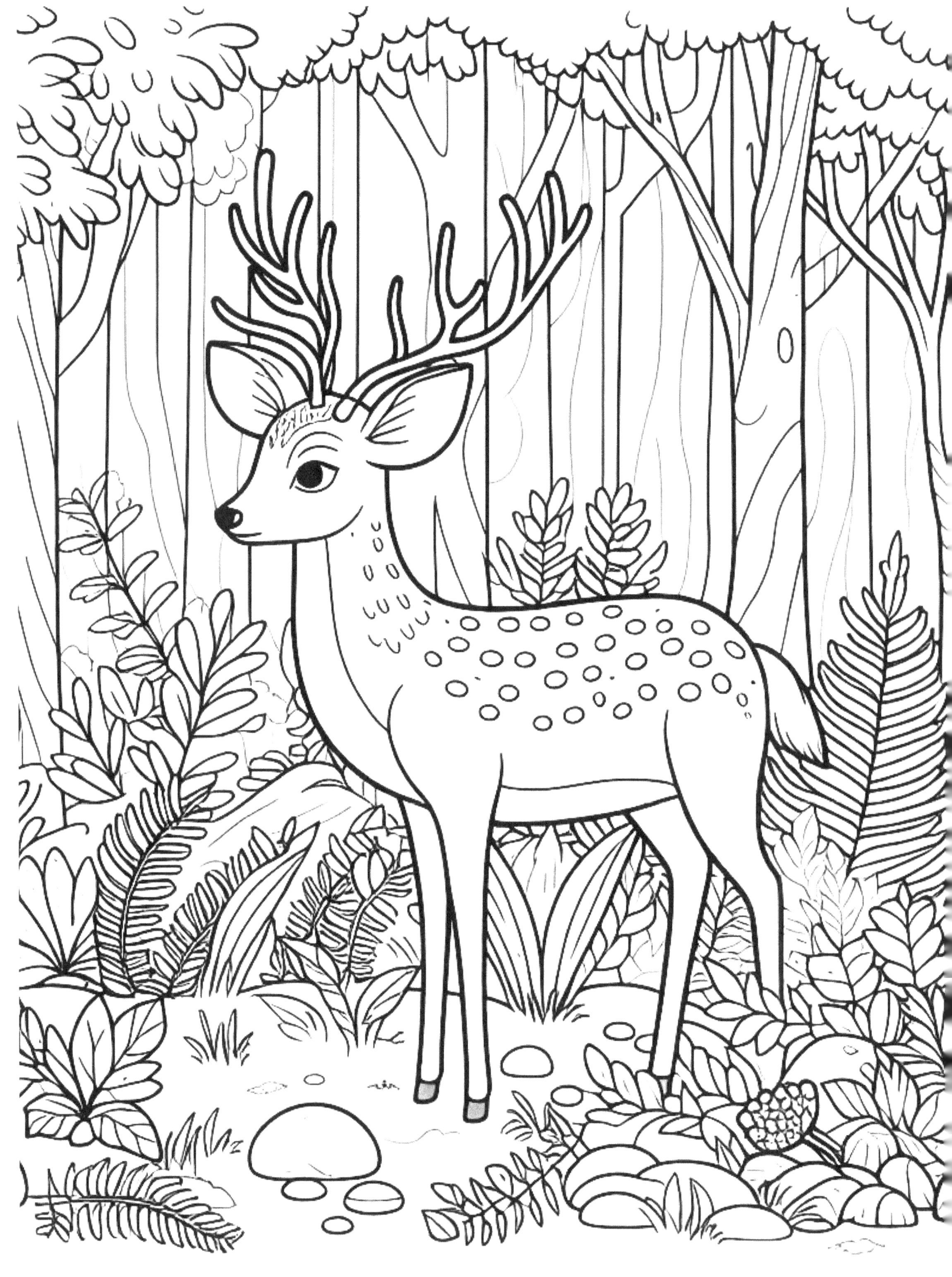

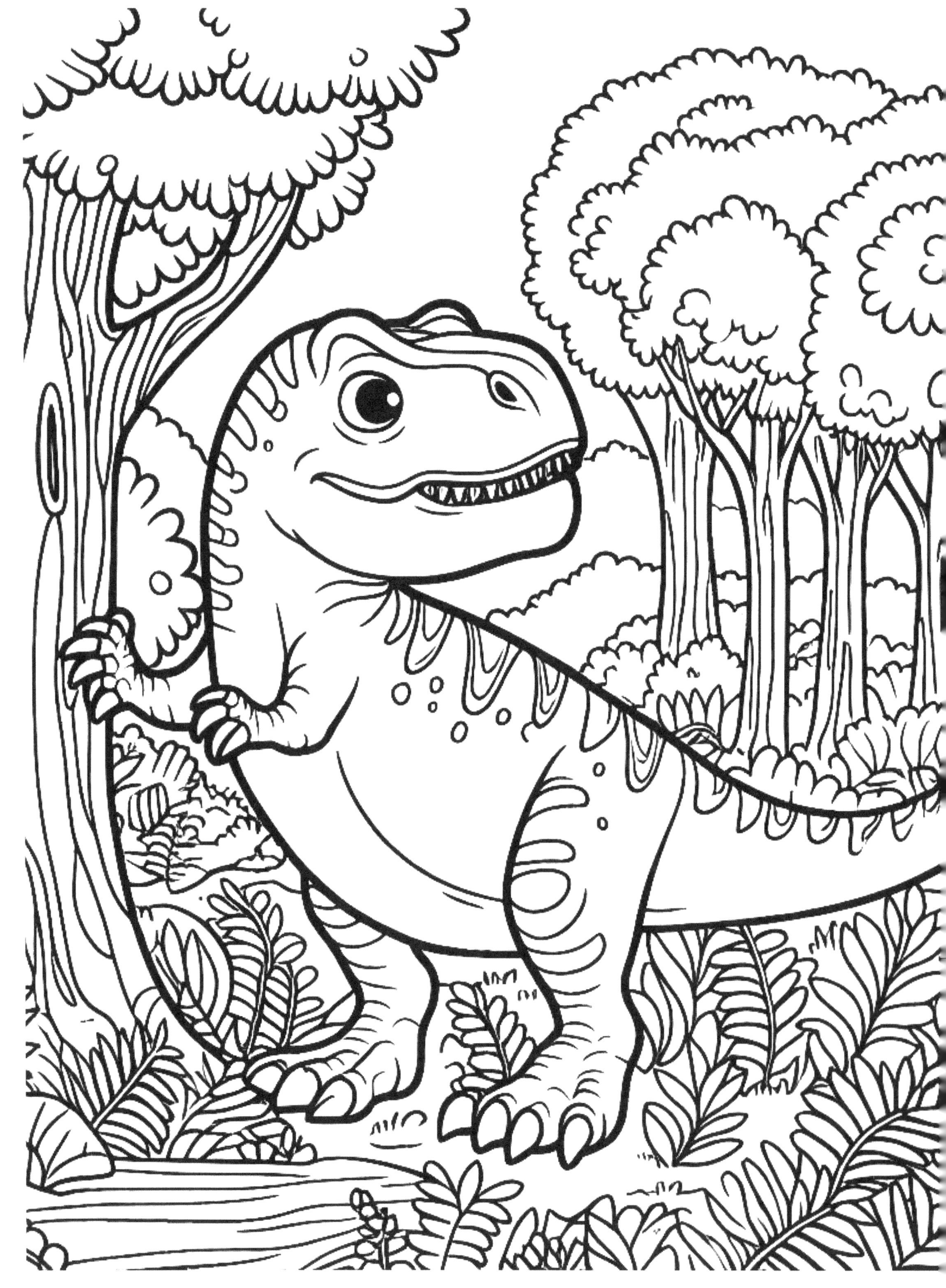

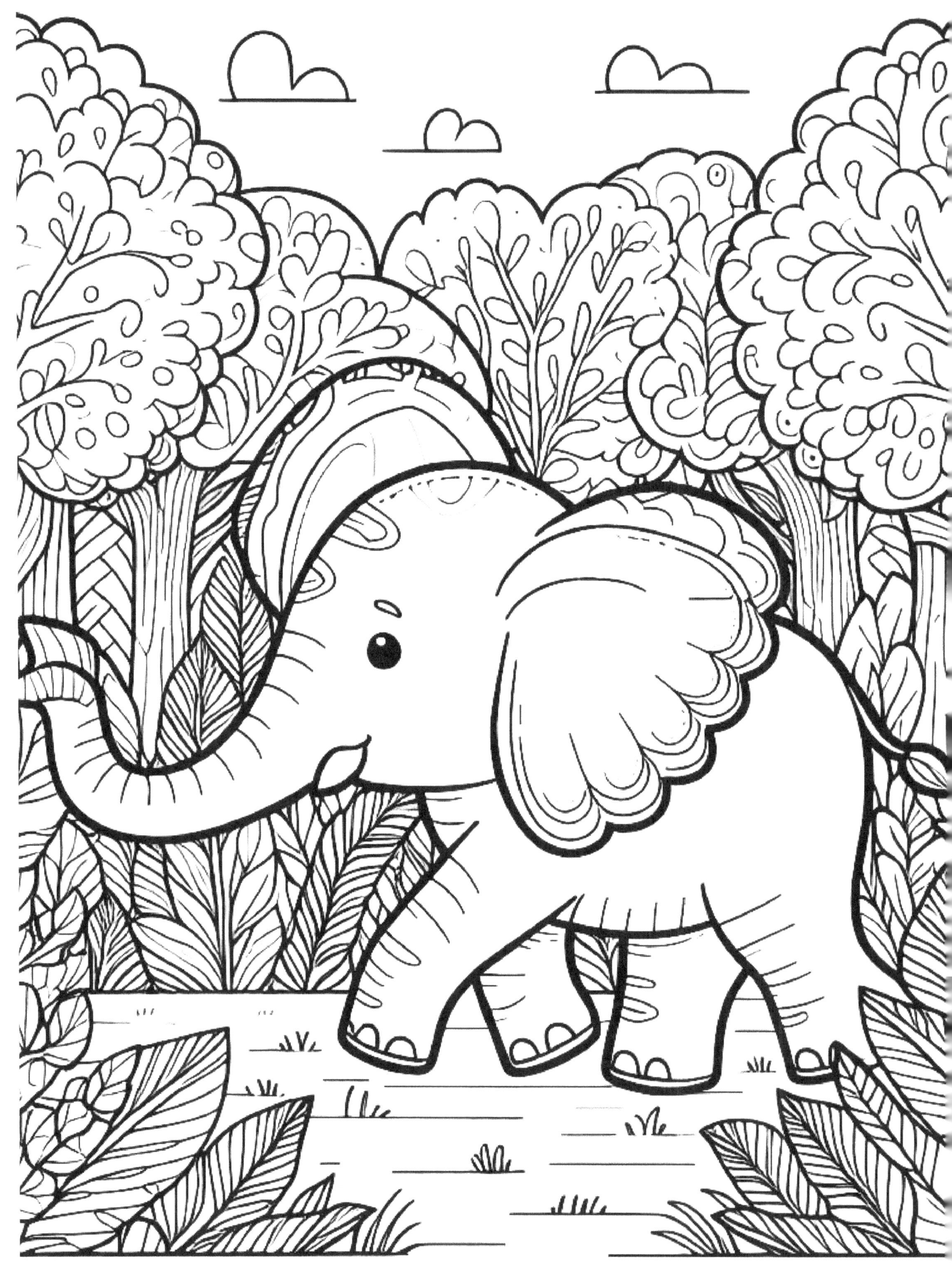

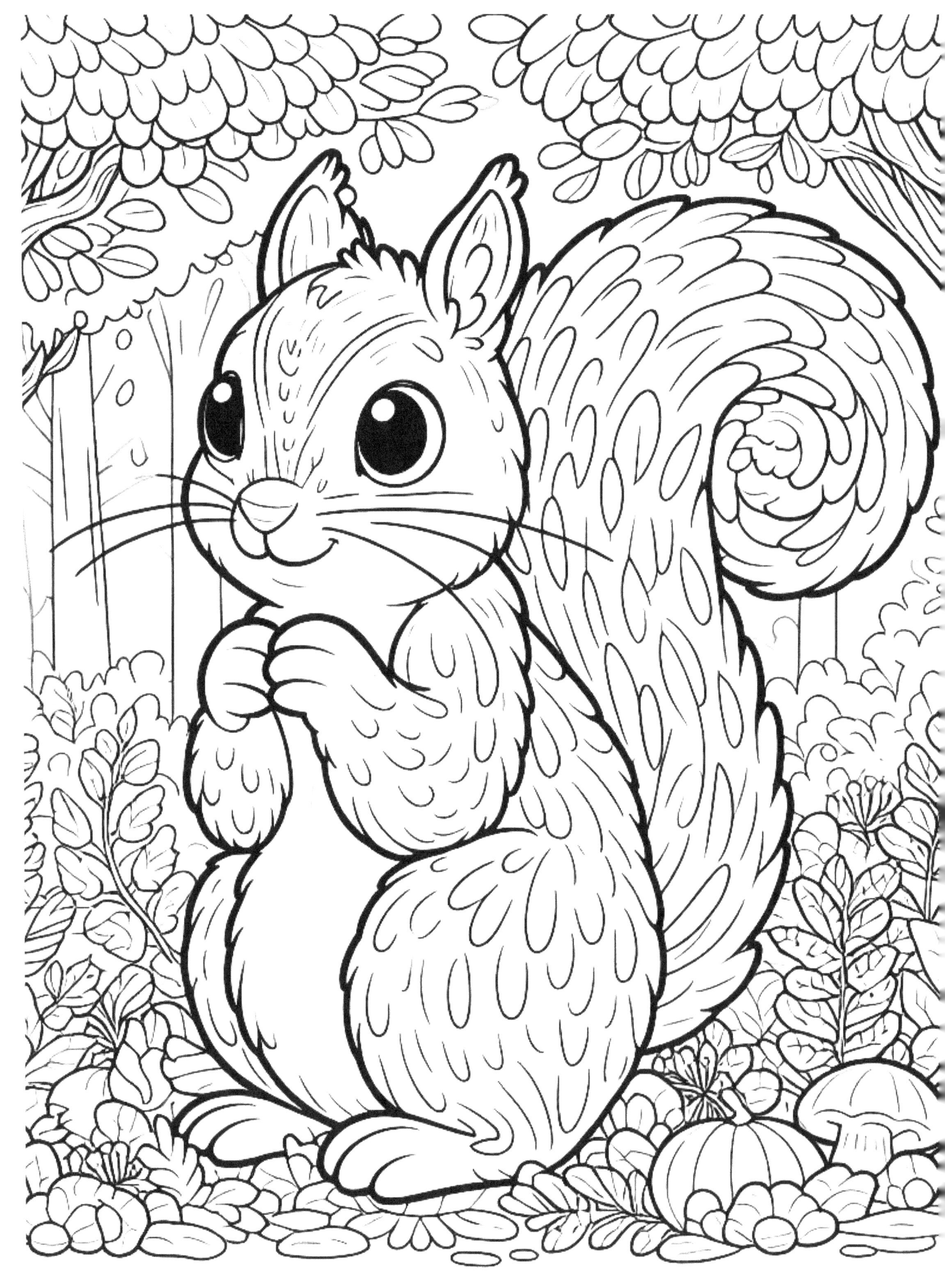

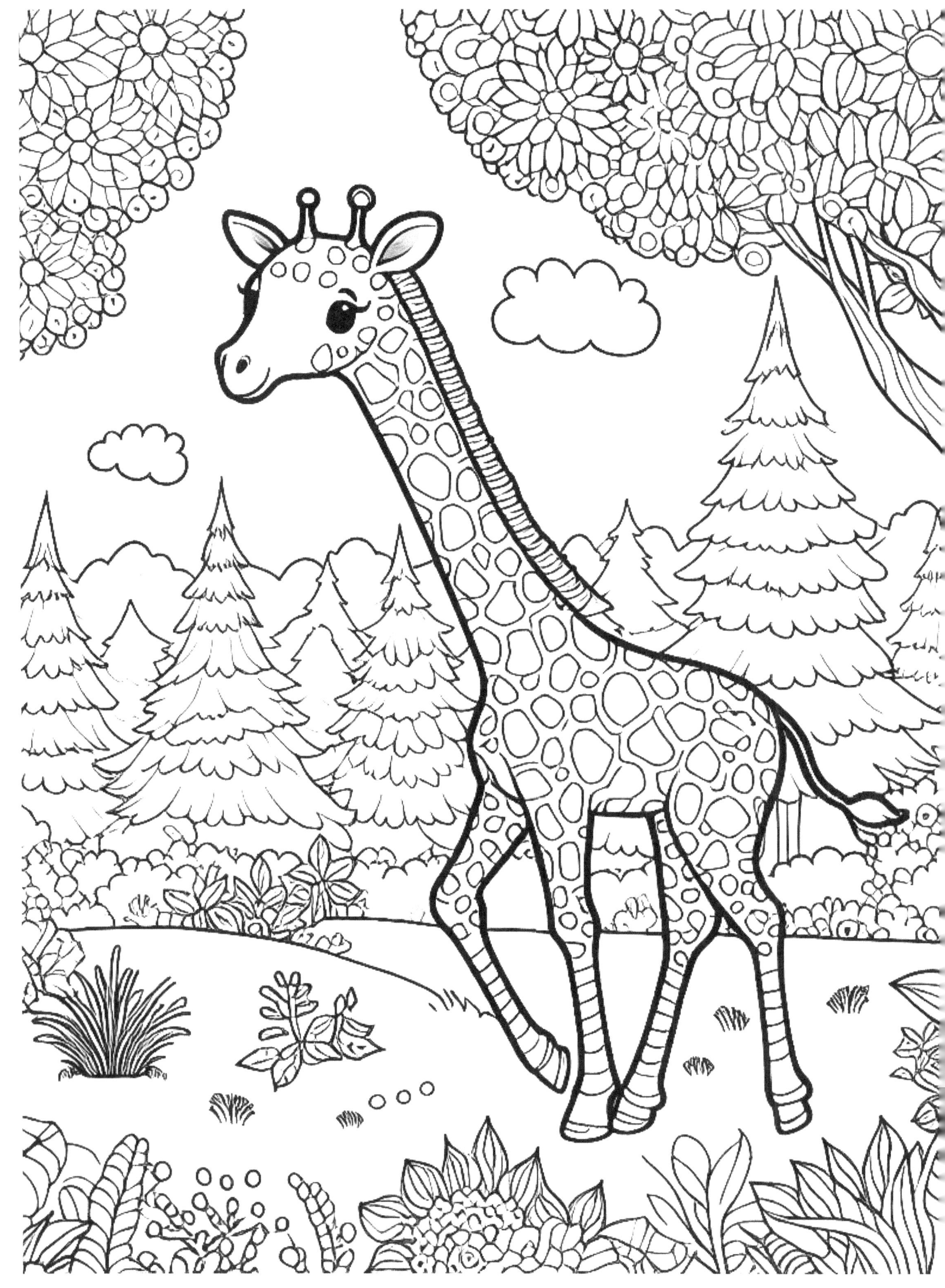

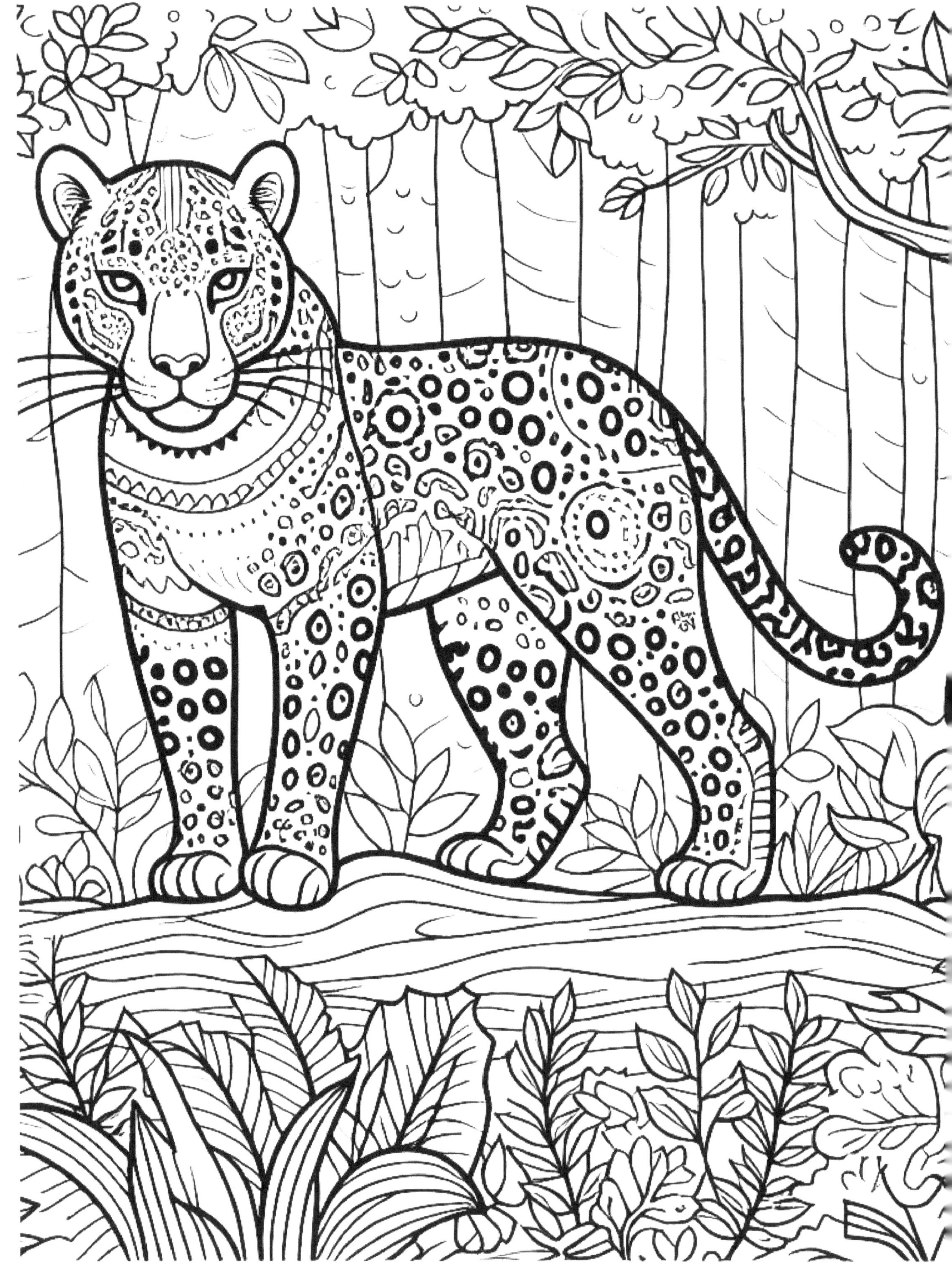

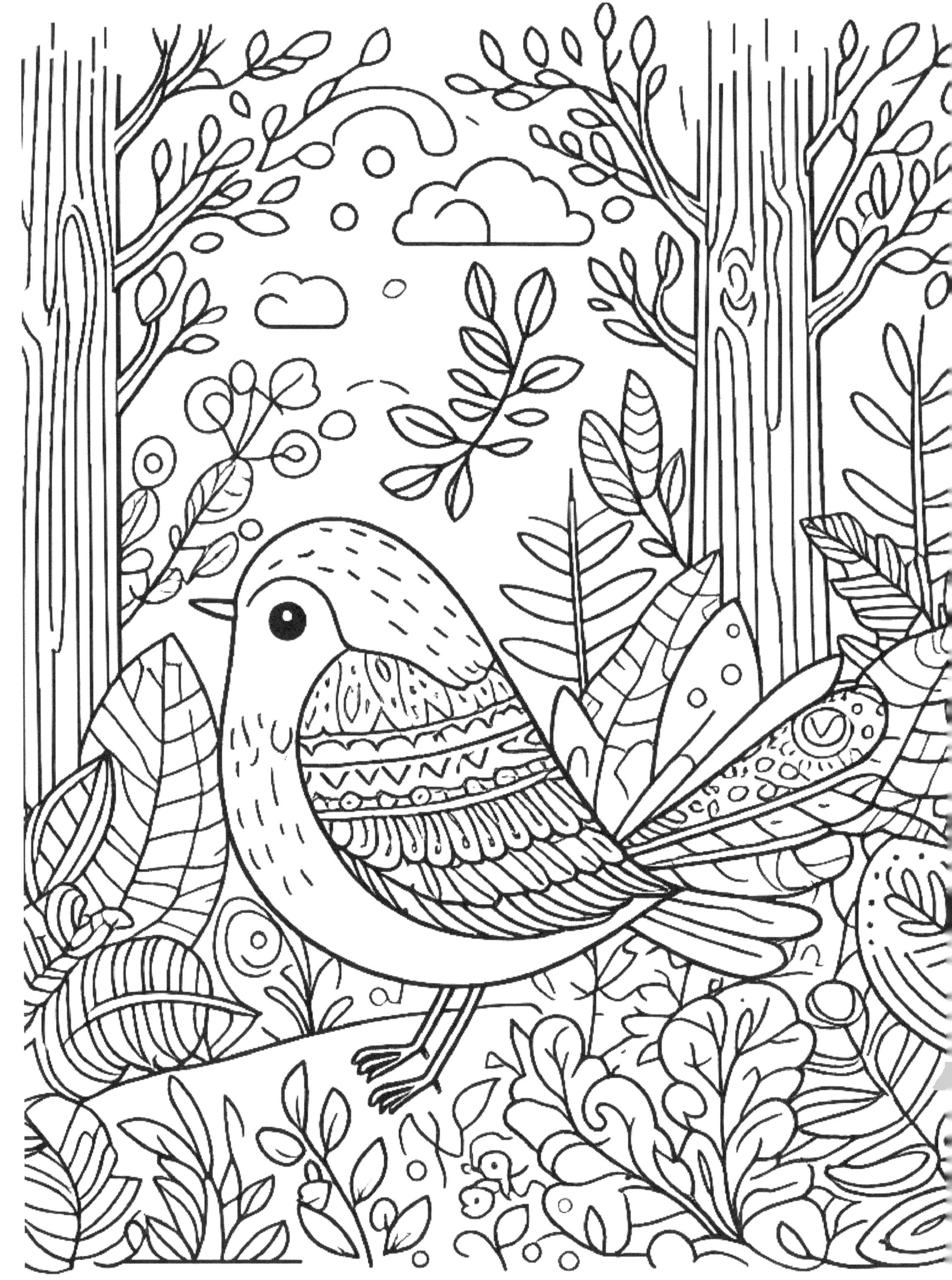

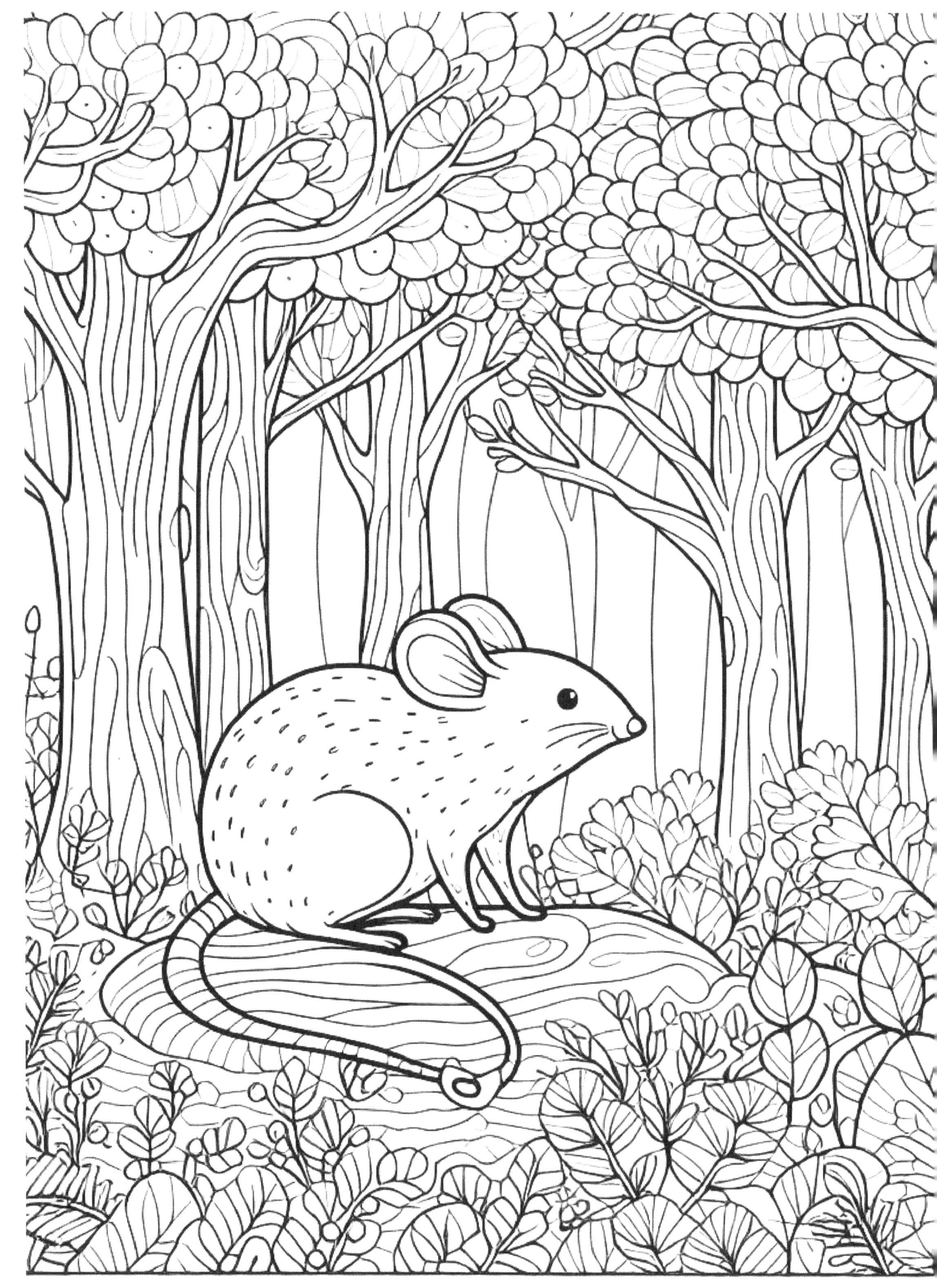

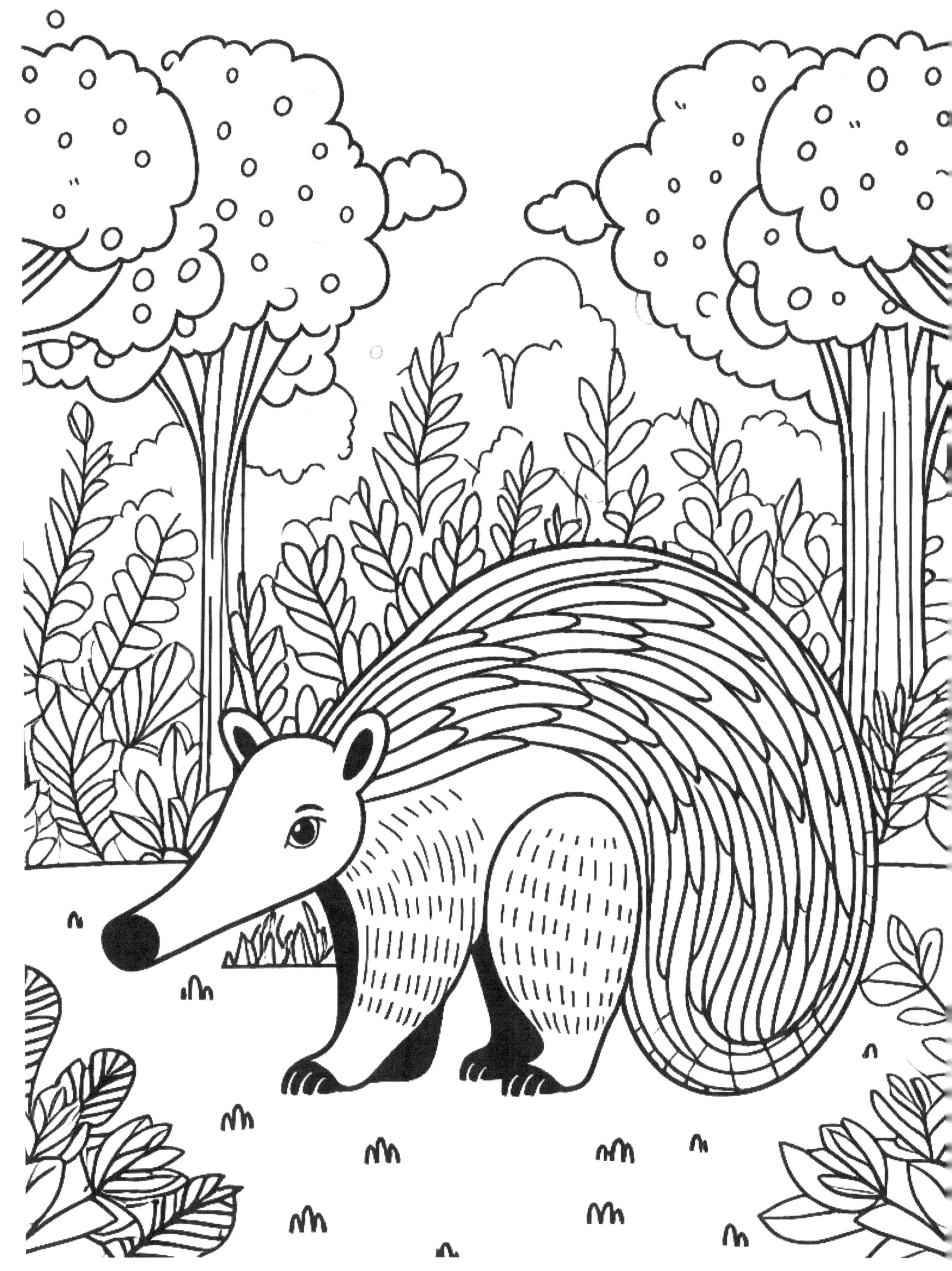

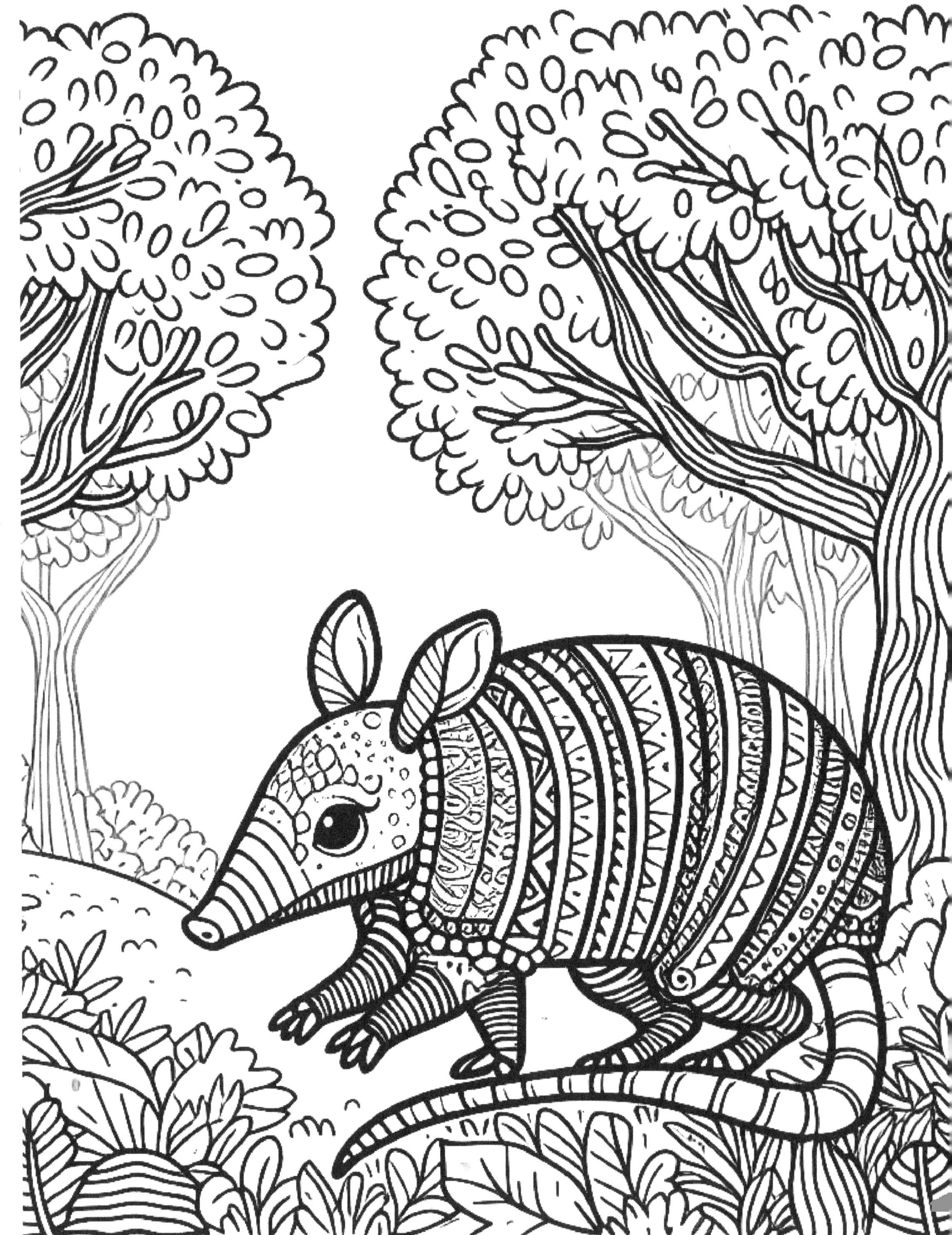

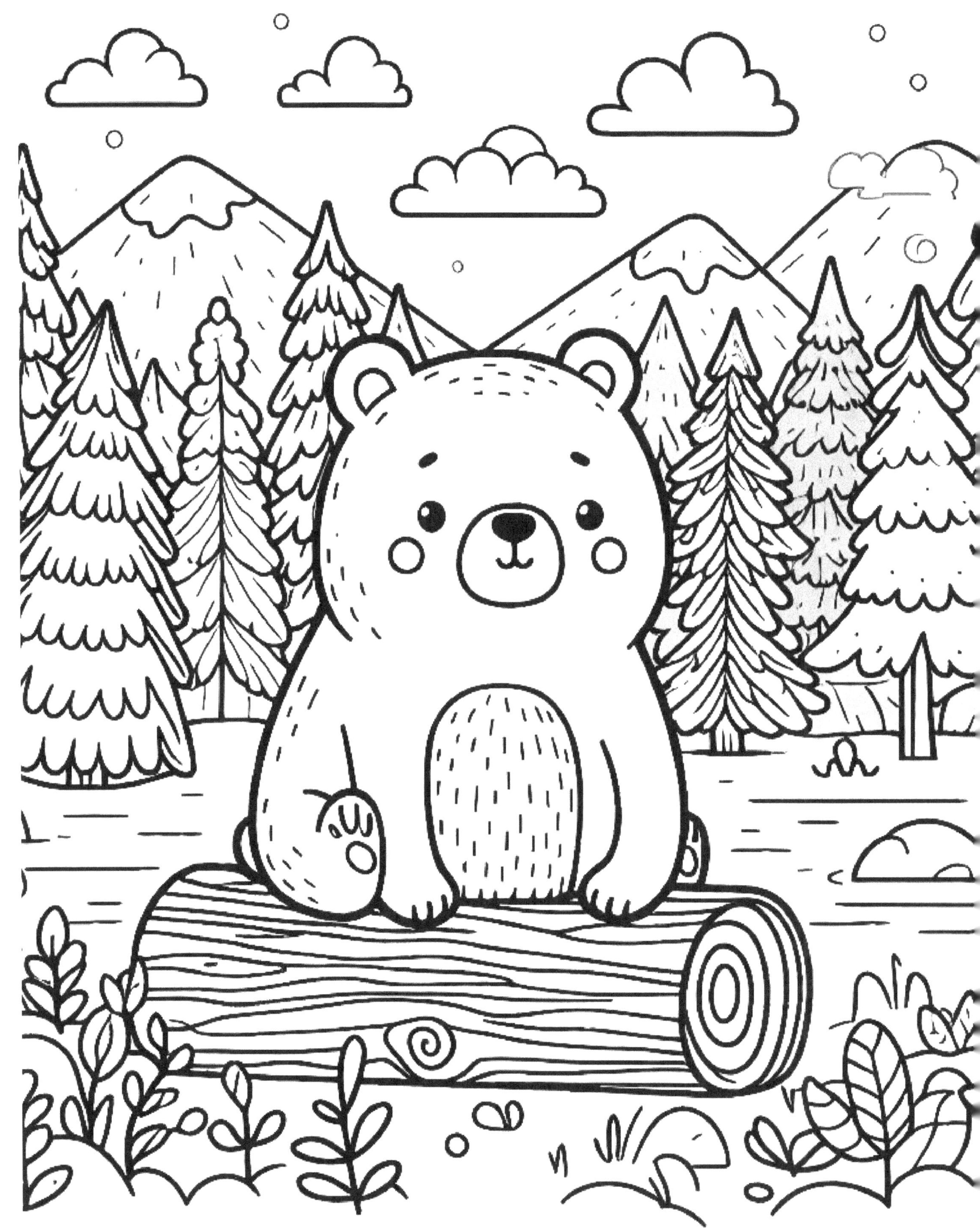

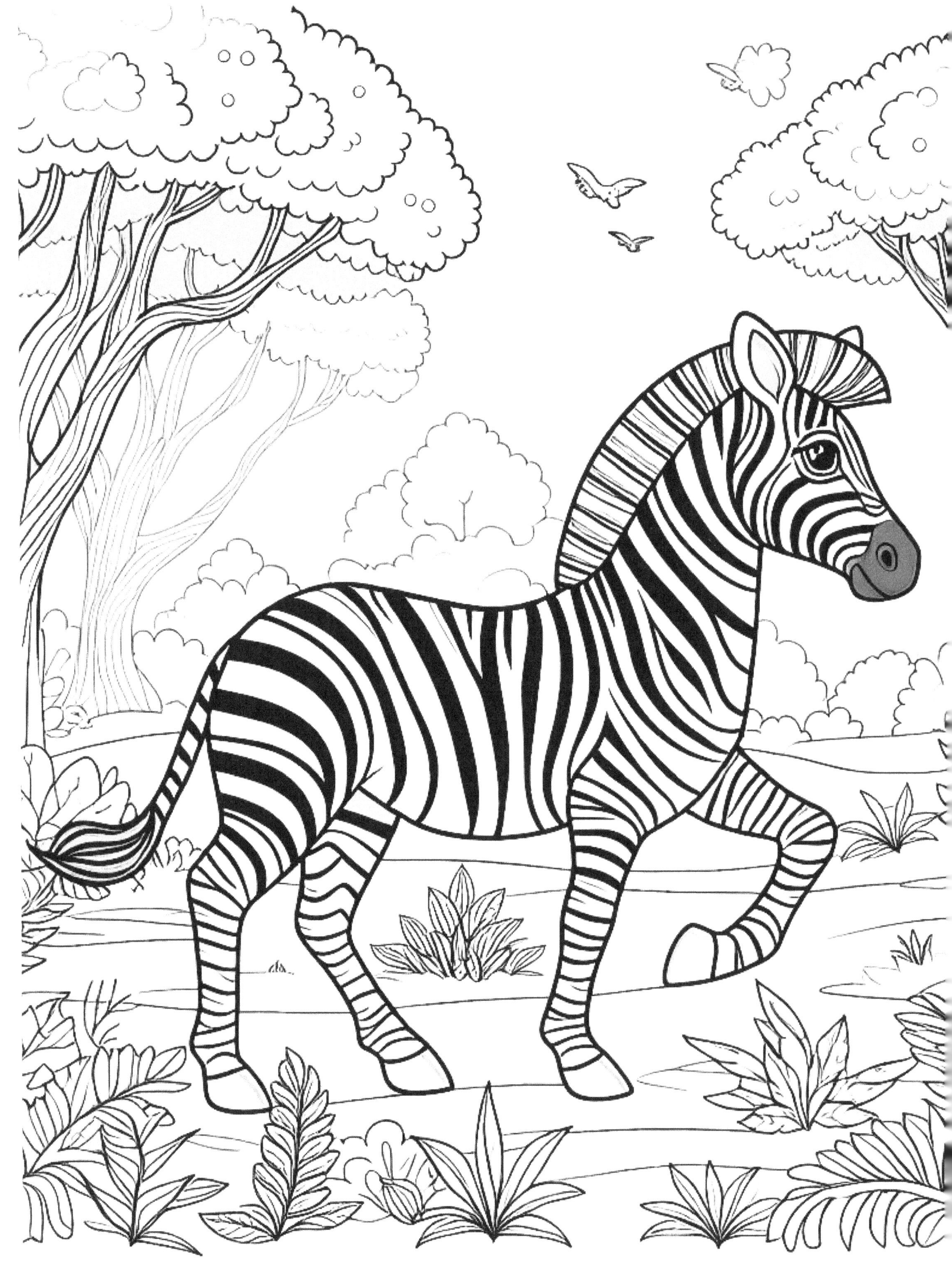

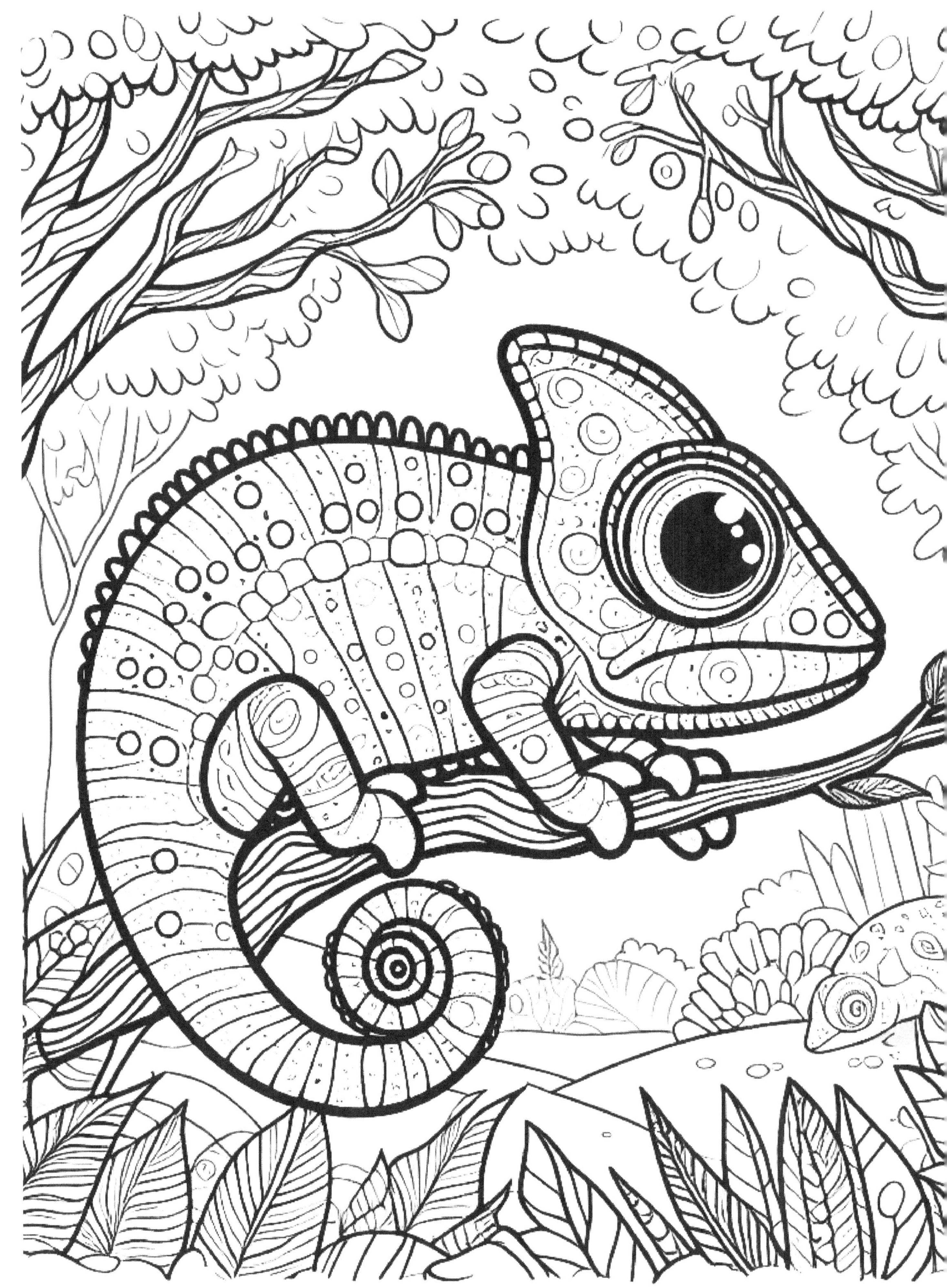

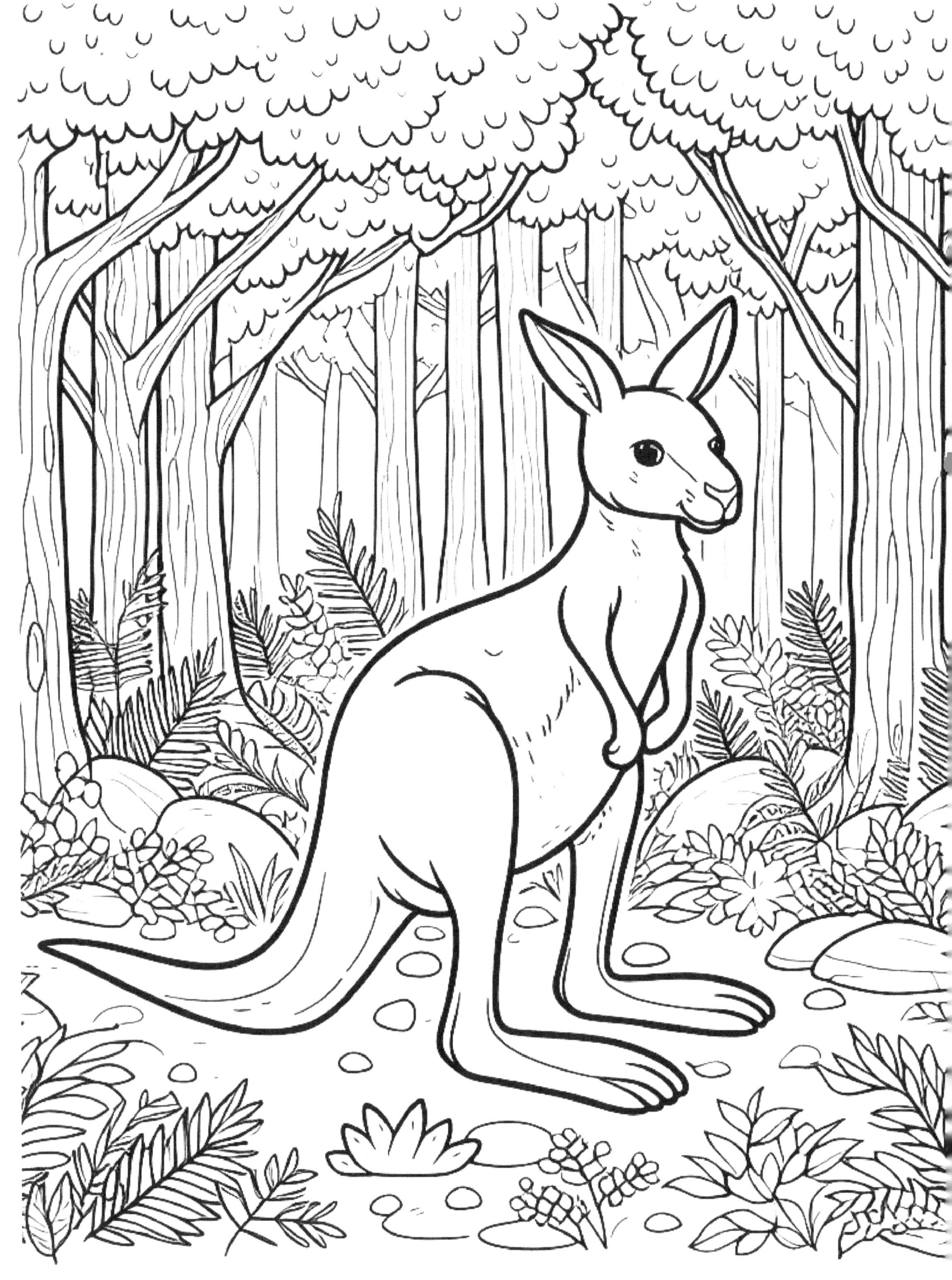

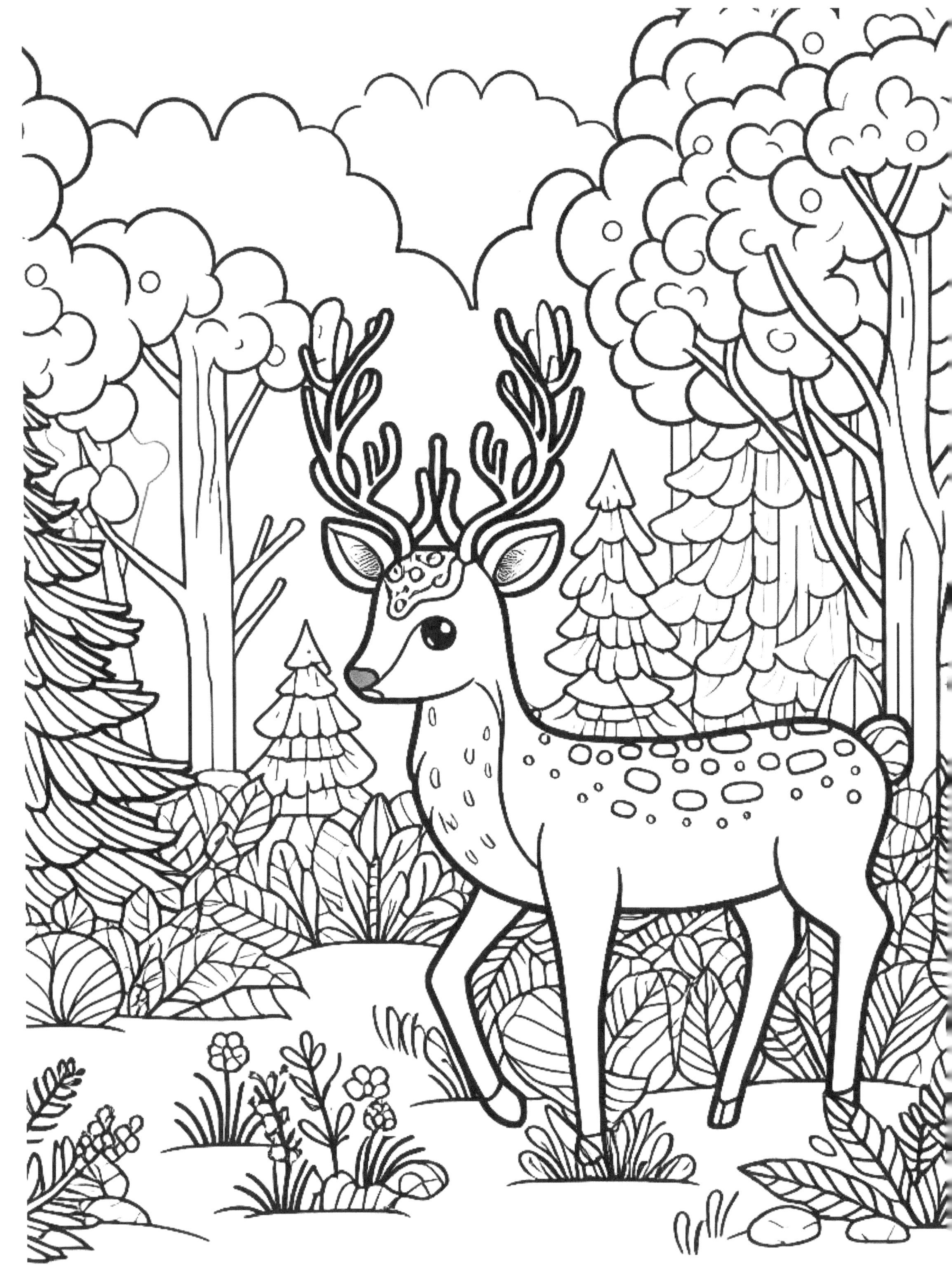

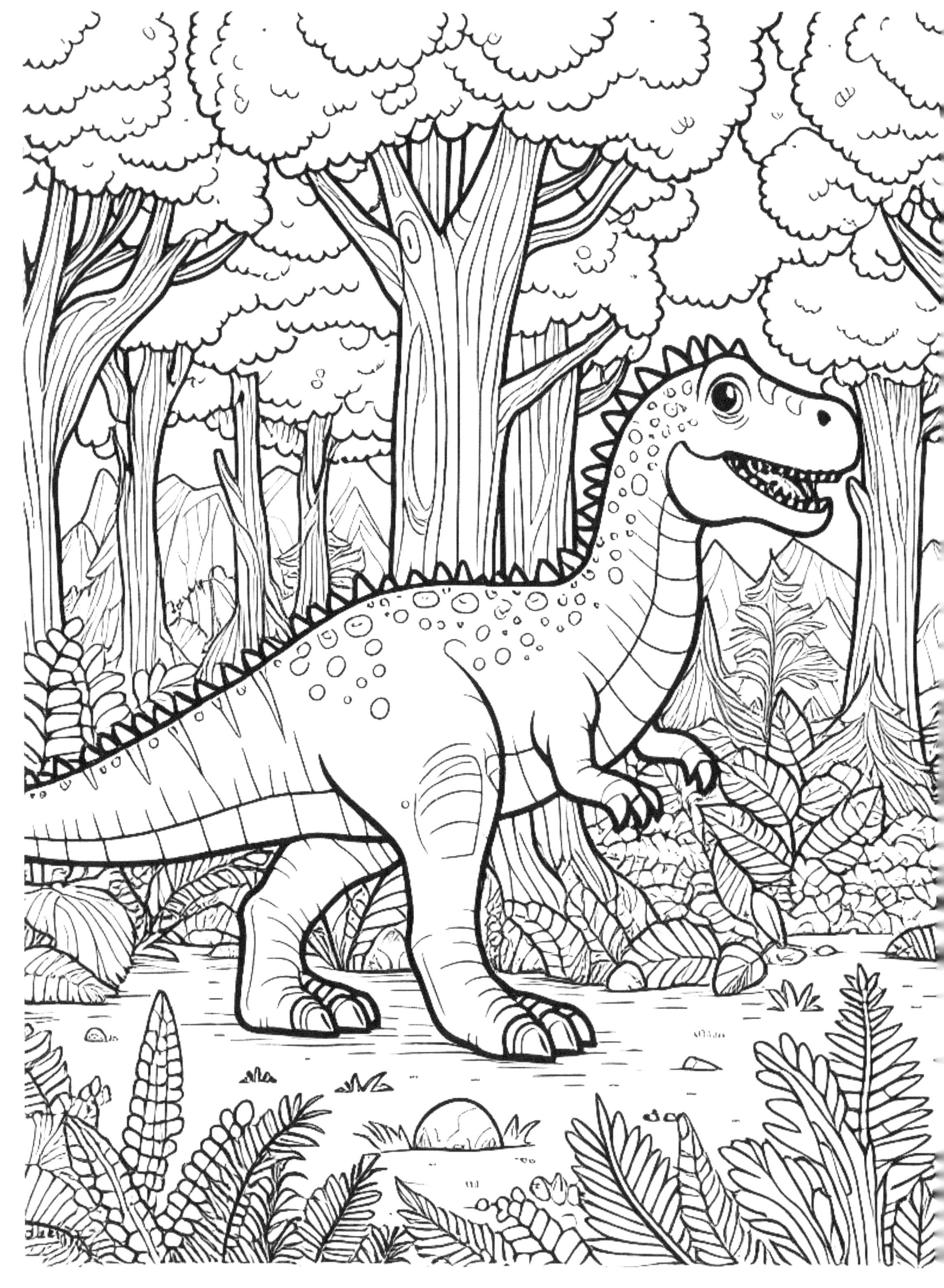

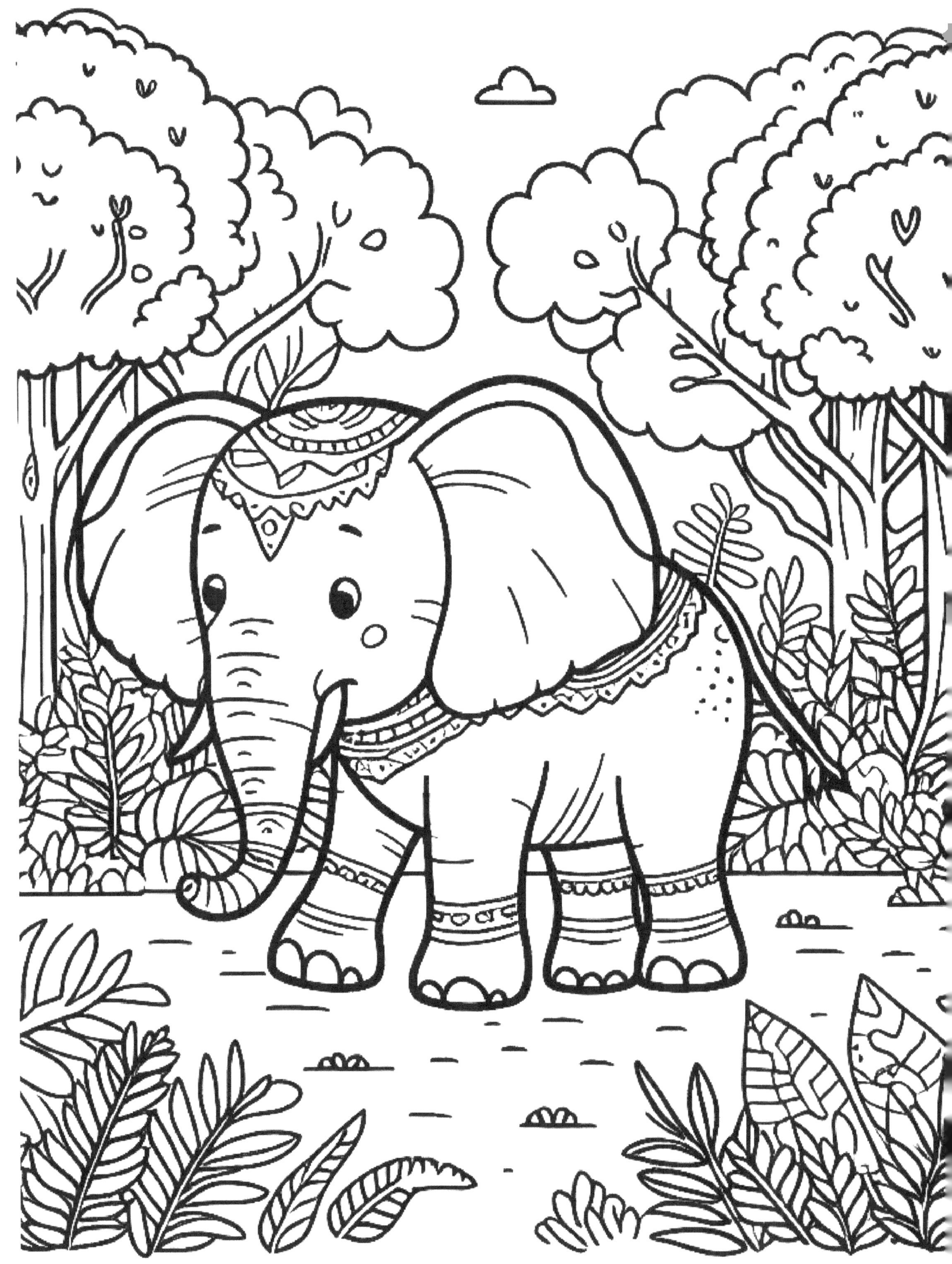

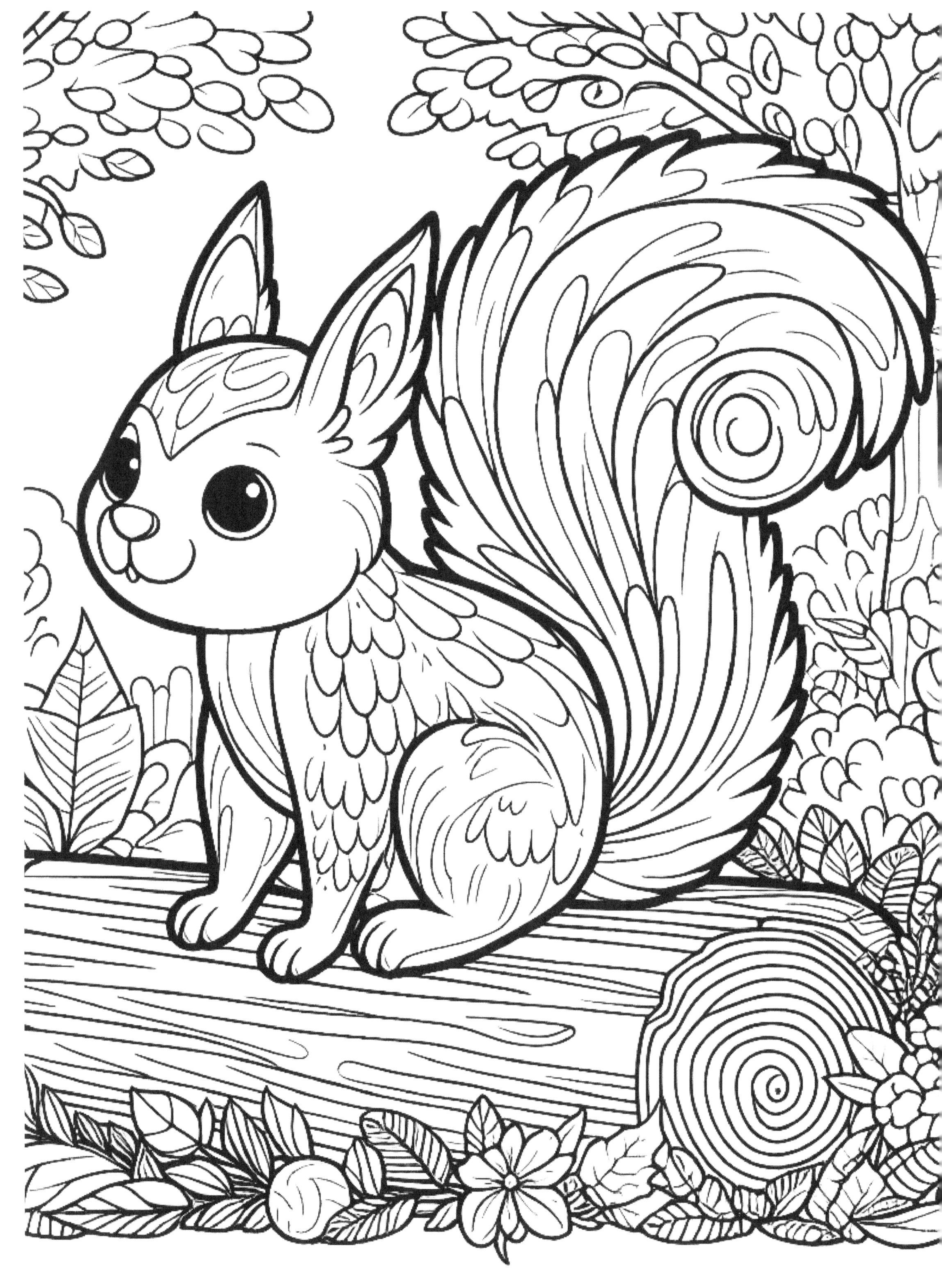

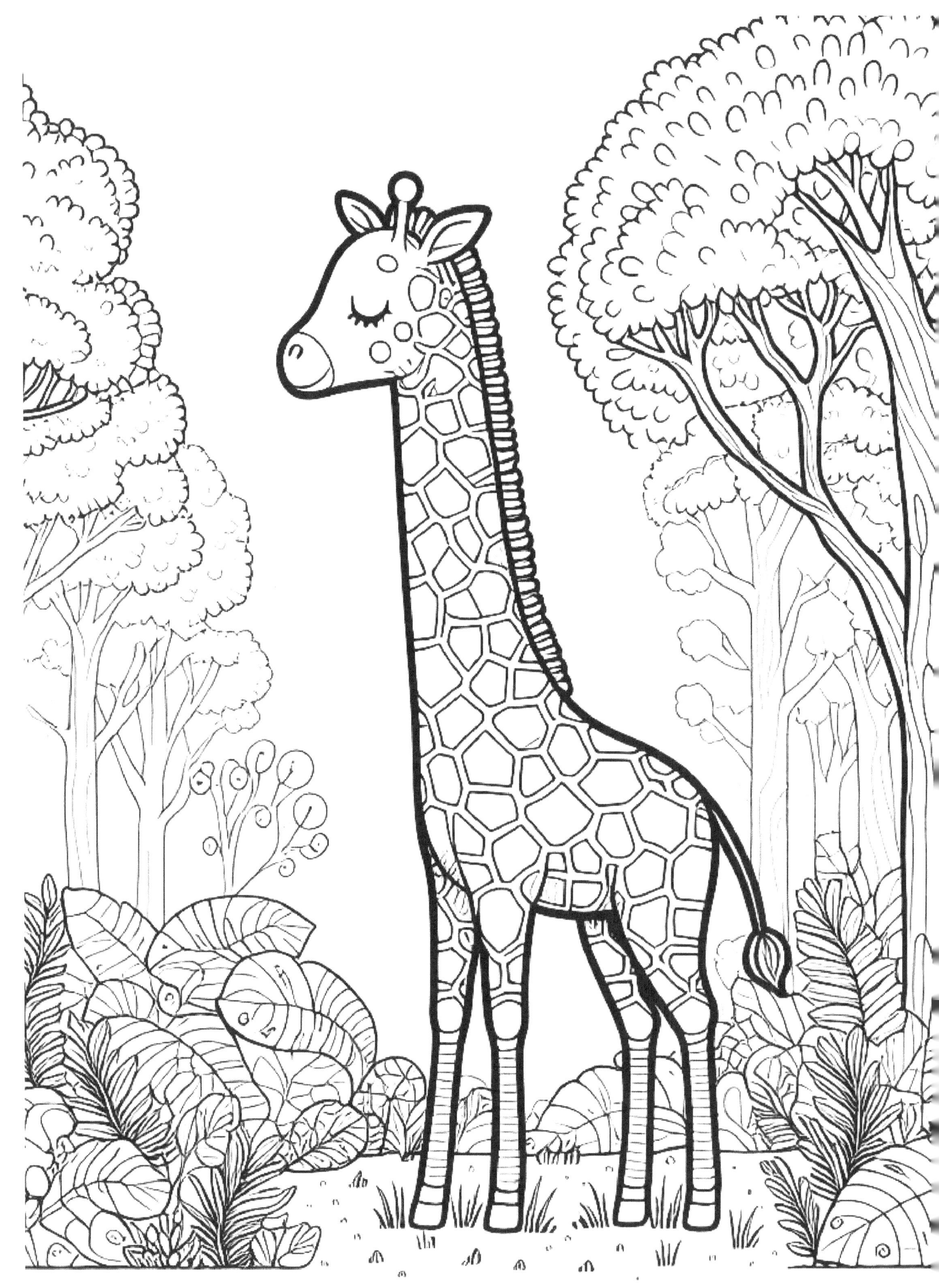

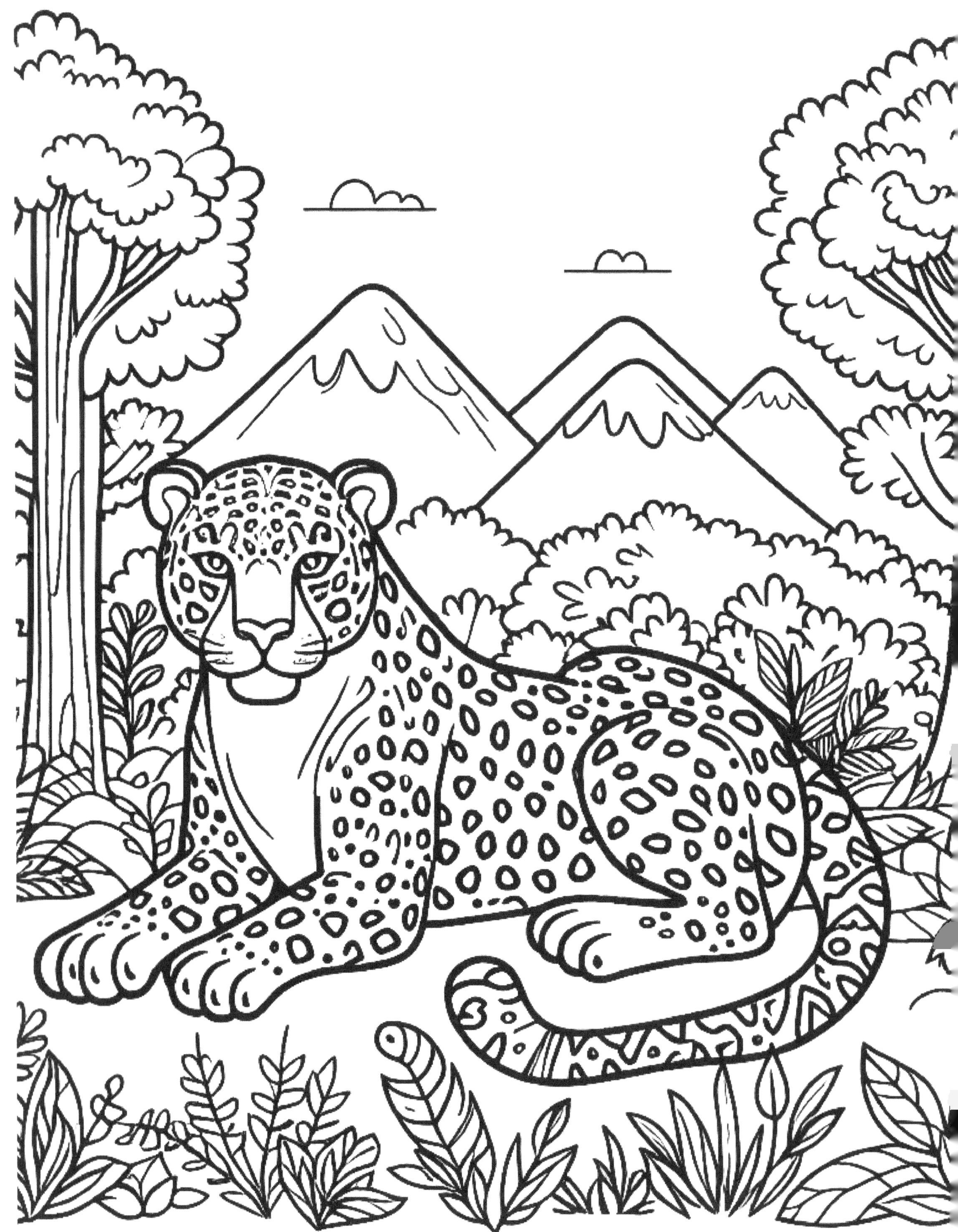

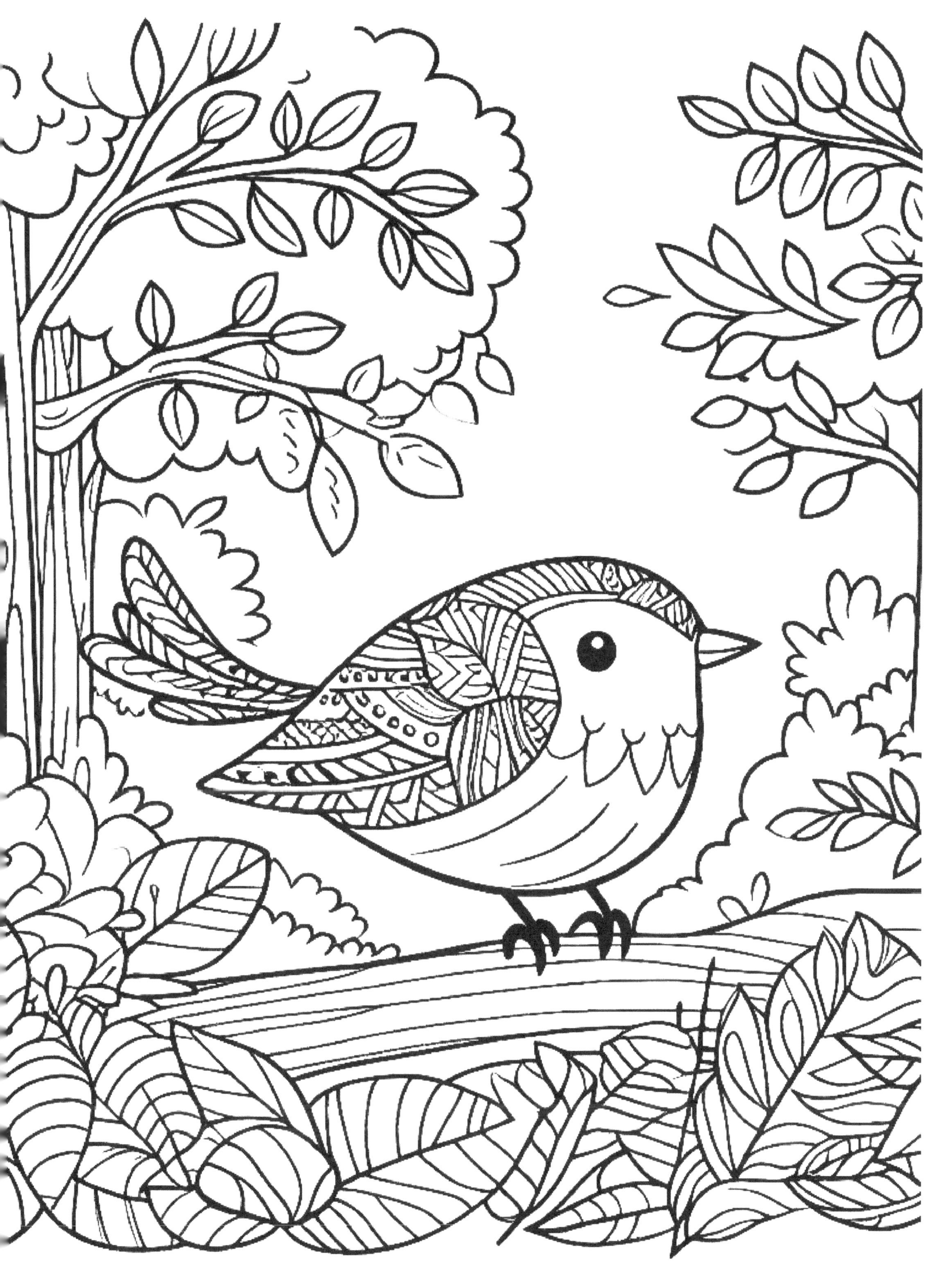

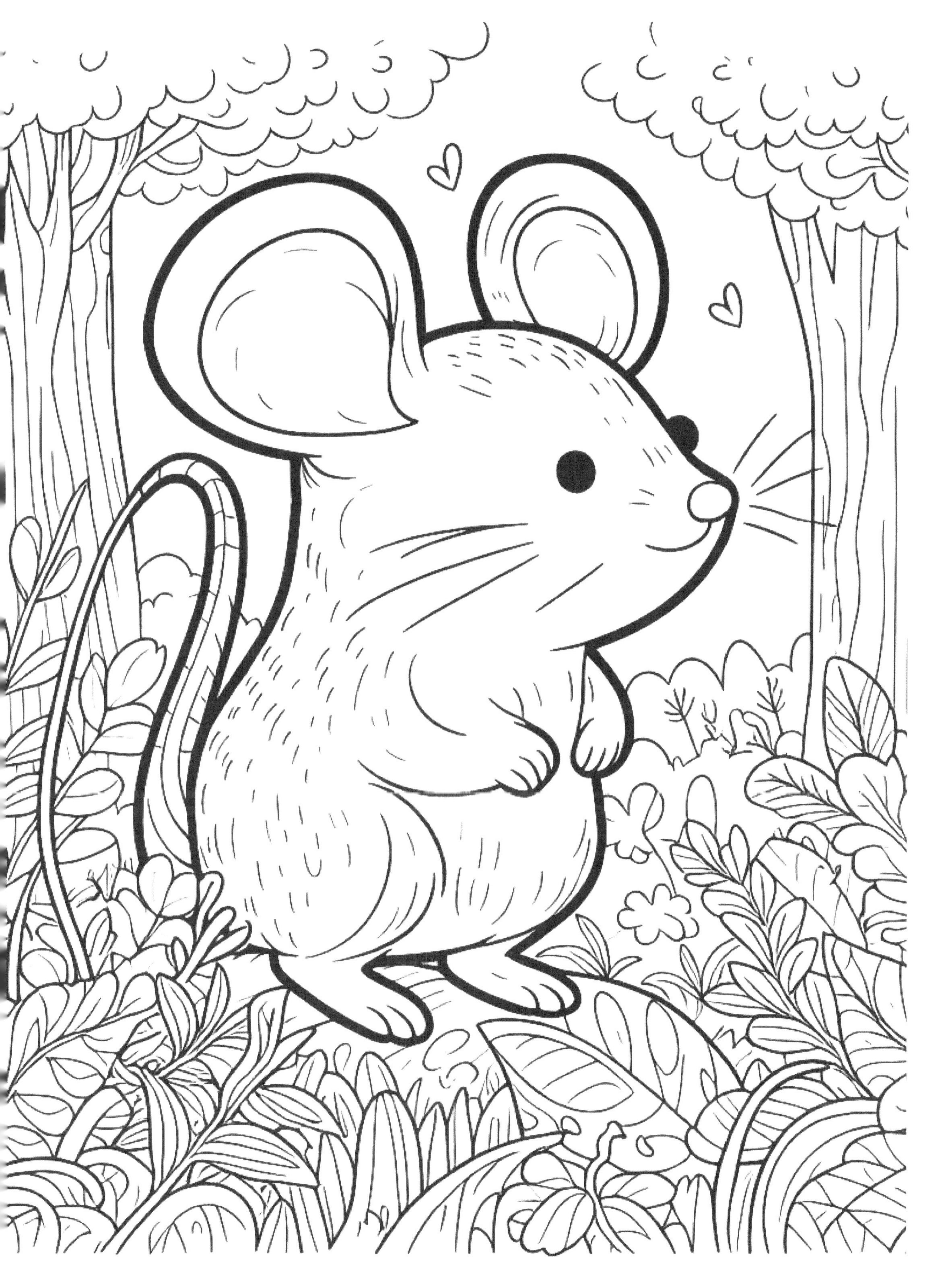

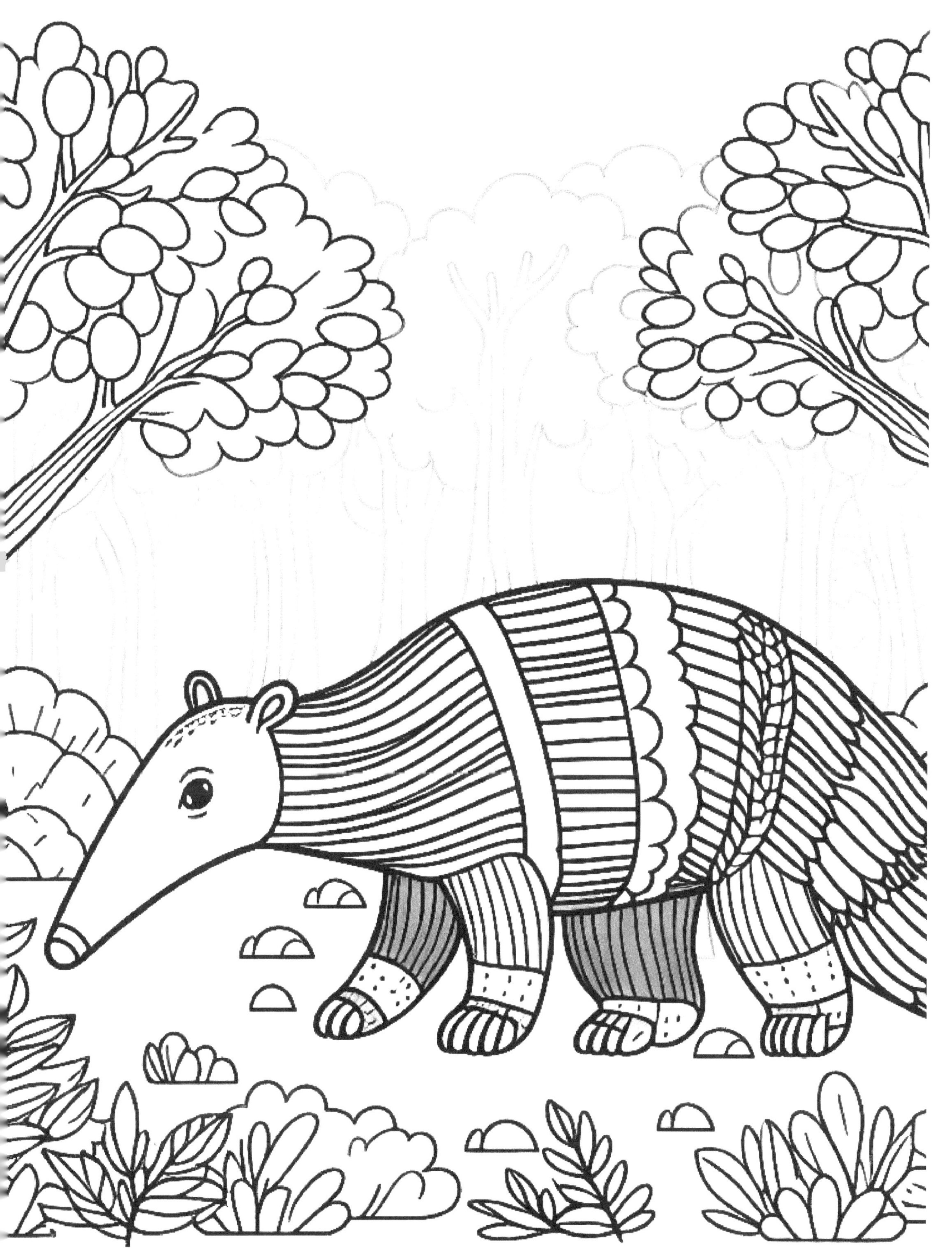

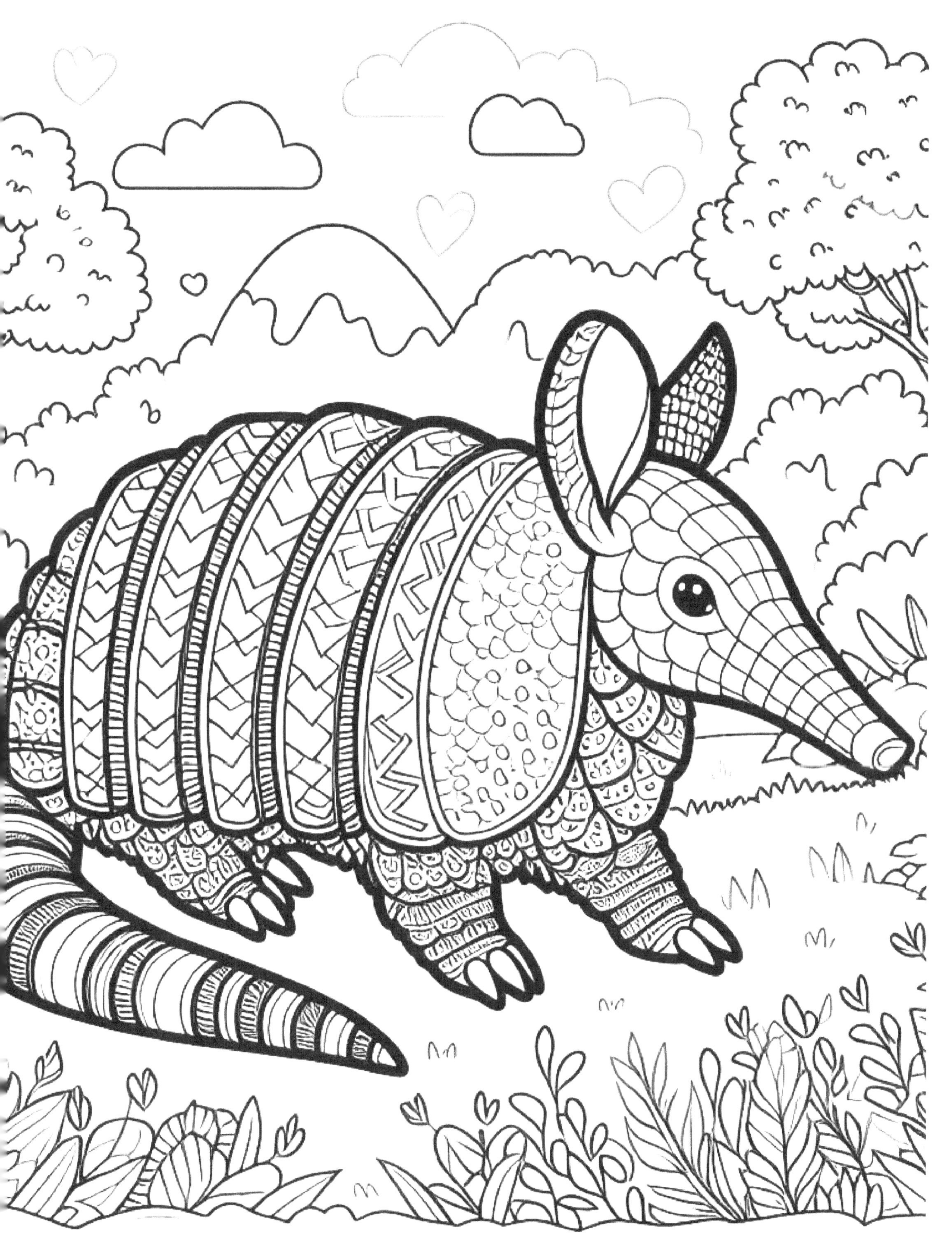

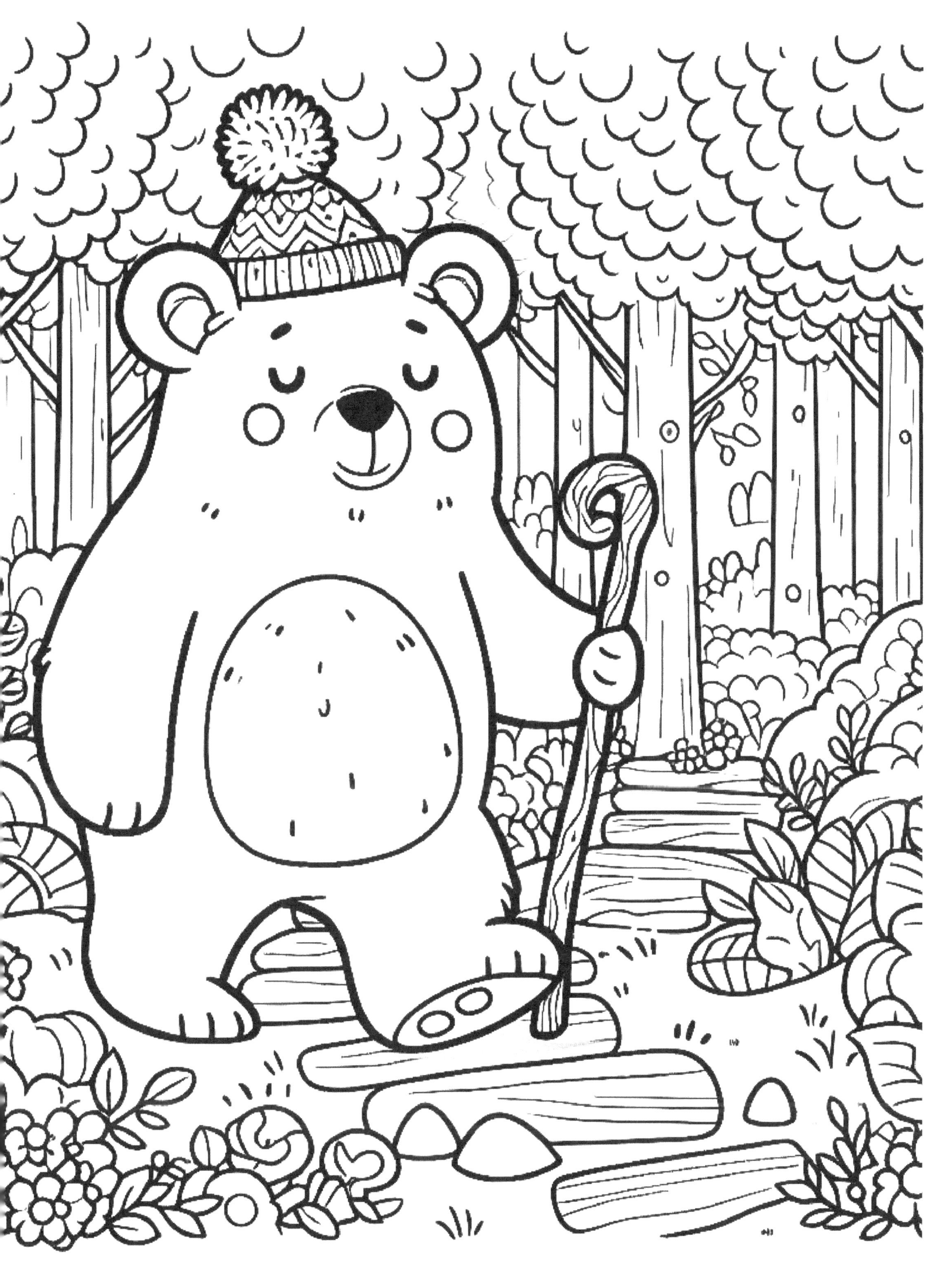

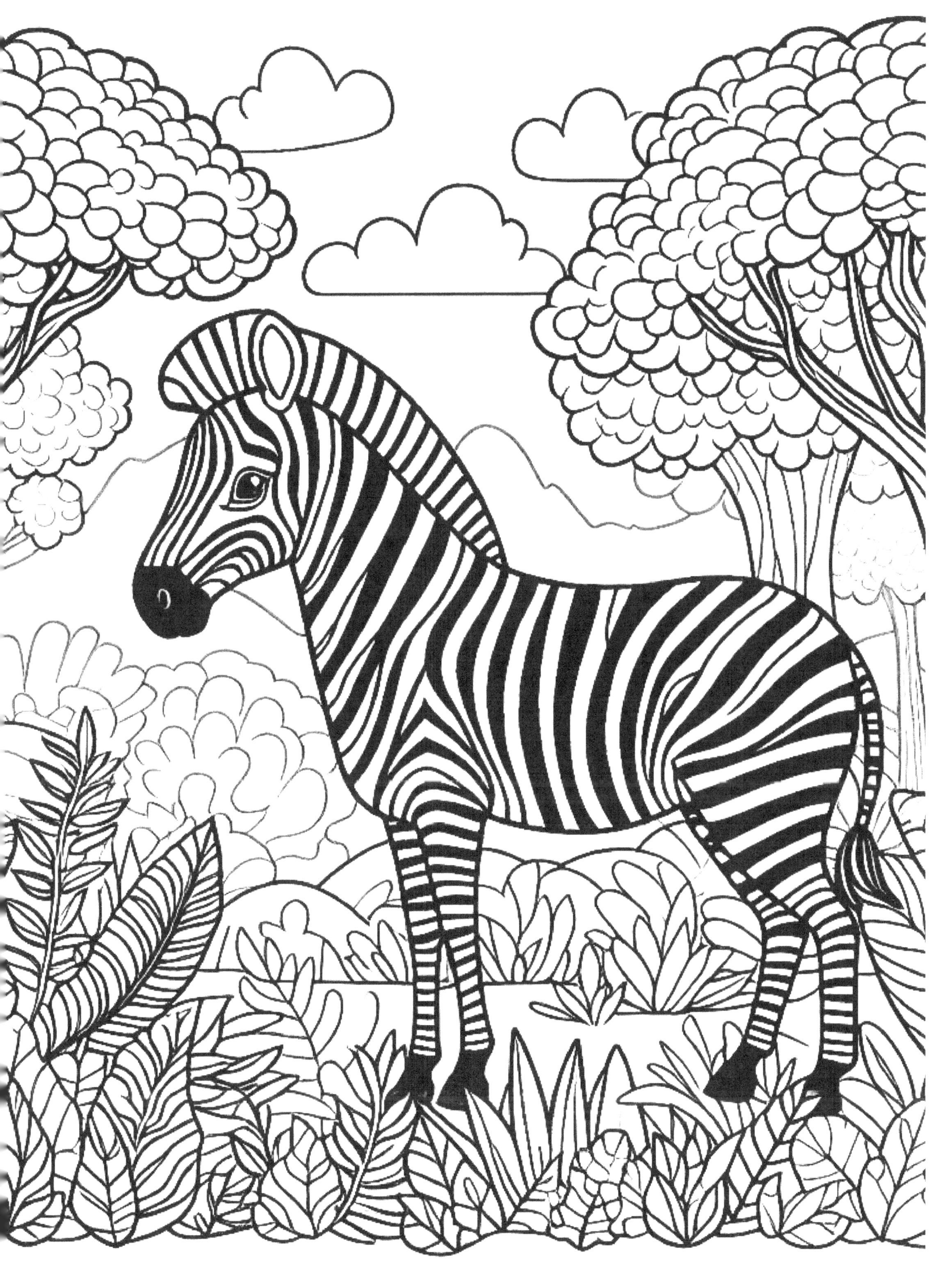

www.ingramcontent.com/pod-product-compliance
Lightning Source LLC
Chambersburg PA
CBHW080240260726
48658CB00008B/3183